This journal belongs to

Jad_leigh.

Understanding My Anxiety

What situations make me anxious?

_____

_____

_____

_____

What do I think and feel in these situations?

_____

_____

_____

_____

How is this thinking distorted?

_____

_____

_____

_____

What is the reality of the situation?

_____

_____

_____

_____

What can I do to change my anxiety levels during these situations?

_____

_____

_____

_____

Self Care Checklist Ideas

Pray / Meditate
Do something creative
Phone a family member or friend
Listen to my favorite music
Listen to a podcast
Read a book
Take a bubble bath
Take a walk
Play with my pets
Memorize a Bible verse or Quote
Doodle / Color In
Get my hair and nails done
Write in my journal
Review my goals
Practice my hobby
Go to gym
Eat a healthy meal
Drink a glass of water
Take a nap
List the things that make me happy
List what I am grateful for
Practice breathing exercises

Anxiety Reducers

What activities and things help you to reduce your anxiety and relax?

_____   _____

_____   _____

_____   _____

_____   _____

_____   _____

_____   _____

_____   _____

_____   _____

_____   _____

_____   _____

_____   _____

_____   _____

_____   _____

_____   _____

_____   _____

_____   _____

_____   _____

_____   _____

_____   _____

My Life Goals

GOAL	By when
ACTION STEPS REQUIRED	REWARD

GOAL	By when
ACTION STEPS REQUIRED	REWARD

GOAL	By when
ACTION STEPS REQUIRED	REWARD

My Goals for Overcoming Anxiety

MY BEHAVIOURS		
Increase	Reduce or Stop	How this will make me behave differently

MY THOUGHTS		
Increase	Reduce or Stop	How this will make me think differently

MY FEELINGS AND EMOTIONS		
Increase	Reduce or Stop	How this will make me feel differently

Monthly Habit Track [MONTH]

HABIT							
	1	2	3	4	5	6	7
	8	9	10	11	12	13	14
REWARD	15	16	17	18	19	20	21
	22	23	24	25	26	27	28
	29	30	31				

HABIT							
	1	2	3	4	5	6	7
	8	9	10	11	12	13	14
REWARD	15	16	17	18	19	20	21
	22	23	24	25	26	27	28
	29	30	31				

HABIT							
	1	2	3	4	5	6	7
	8	9	10	11	12	13	14
REWARD	15	16	17	18	19	20	21
	22	23	24	25	26	27	28
	29	30	31				

NOTES

Symptom Tracker

	Panic Attack	No Appetite	Insomnia	Head-ache	Heart Rate Up	GI Dis-comfort	Sweaty Palms	
1								
2								
3								
4								
5								
6								
7								
8								
9								
10								
11								
12								
13								
14								
15								
16								
17								
18								
19								
20								
21								
22								
23								
24								
25								
26								
27								
28								
29								
30								
31								

Monthly Anxiety Track

MONTH					
	1 Low	2	3	4	5 High
1					
2					
3					
4					
5					
6					
7					
8					
9					
10					
11					
12					
13					
14					
15					
16					
17					
18					
19					
20					
21					
22					
23					
24					
25					
26					
27					
28					
29					
30					
31					

Symptom Tracker

MONTH

	Panic Attack	No Appetite	Insomnia	Head-ache	Heart Rate Up	GI Dis-comfort	Sweaty Palms	
1								
2								
3								
4								
5								
6								
7								
8								
9								
10								
11								
12								
13								
14								
15								
16								
17								
18								
19								
20								
21								
22								
23								
24								
25								
26								
27								
28								
29								
30								
31								

Monthly Anxiety Track

	MONTH				
	1 Low	2	3	4	5 High
1					
2					
3					
4					
5					
6					
7					
8					
9					
10					
11					
12					
13					
14					
15					
16					
17					
18					
19					
20					
21					
22					
23					
24					
25					
26					
27					
28					
29					
30					
31					

Symptom Tracker

	Panic Attack	No Appetite	Insomnia	Head-ache	Heart Rate Up	GI Dis-comfort	Sweaty Palms	
1								
2								
3								
4								
5								
6								
7								
8								
9								
10								
11								
12								
13								
14								
15								
16								
17								
18								
19								
20								
21								
22								
23								
24								
25								
26								
27								
28								
29								
30								
31								

Monthly Anxiety Track

	1 Low	2	3	4	5 High
MONTH					
1					
2					
3					
4					
5					
6					
7					
8					
9					
10					
11					
12					
13					
14					
15					
16					
17					
18					
19					
20					
21					
22					
23					
24					
25					
26					
27					
28					
29					
30					
31					

"Anxiety's like a rocking chair.
It gives you something to do,
but it doesn't get you very far."
~ Jodi Picoult

Weekly Anxiety Tracker

MONDAY

Overall Anxiety Level									
1	2	3	4	5	6	7	8	9	10
Low									High

Overall Mood									
1	2	3	4	5	6	7	8	9	10
Very Bad									Excellent

TUESDAY

Overall Anxiety Level									
1	2	3	4	5	6	7	8	9	10
Low									High

Overall Mood									
1	2	3	4	5	6	7	8	9	10
Very Bad									Excellent

WEDNESDAY

Overall Anxiety Level									
1	2	3	4	5	6	7	8	9	10
Low									High

Overall Mood									
1	2	3	4	5	6	7	8	9	10
Very Bad									Excellent

THURSDAY

Overall Anxiety Level									
1	2	3	4	5	6	7	8	9	10
Low									High

Overall Mood									
1	2	3	4	5	6	7	8	9	10
Very Bad									Excellent

WEEK OF _____ / ____ / ____

FRIDAY	Overall Anxiety Level
	1 2 3 4 5 6 7 8 9 10
	Low High
	Overall Mood
	1 2 3 4 5 6 7 8 9 10
	Very Bad Excellent

SATURDAY	Overall Anxiety Level
	1 2 3 4 5 6 7 8 9 10
	Low High
	Overall Mood
	1 2 3 4 5 6 7 8 9 10
	Very Bad Excellent

SUNDAY	Overall Anxiety Level
	1 2 3 4 5 6 7 8 9 10
	Low High
	Overall Mood
	1 2 3 4 5 6 7 8 9 10
	Very Bad Excellent

NOTES

_____

_____

_____

_____

_____

_____

Self Care Checklist

ACTIVITY	M	T	W	T	F	S	S
SPIRITUAL							
PYSICAL							
MENTAL							

Write a thank you letter to
the people who support you
emotionally and describe
what they do that is
meaningful to you.

DATE: _____ / _____ /
_____

_____

_____

_____

_____

_____

_____

_____

_____

_____

_____

_____

_____

_____

_____

_____

_____

_____

Anxiety Triggers

When this happens:

This is what I think:

This is how I feel:

What I can do in this event to reduce my anxiety:

Anxiety Worksheet

DATE: _____ / _____ / _____

What happened?

What were my thoughts?

How did I handle it?

How did I feel?

What can I do to improve?

Anxiety Worksheet

DATE: _____ / _____ / _____

What happened?

What were my thoughts?	How did I feel?

How did I handle it?

What can I do to improve?

Exercise to Calm Down

B·R·E·A·T·H·E

5 Things I Can See

1.

2.

3.

4.

5.

4 Things I Can Touch

1.

2.

3.

4.

3 Things I Can Hear

1.

2.

3.

2 Things I Can Smell

1.

2.

1 Thing I Can Taste

1.

"Life is
10 percent
what you experience
and
90 percent
how you
respond to it."
~ Dorothy M. Neddermeyer

Weekly Anxiety Tracker

MONDAY

Overall Anxiety Level									
1	2	3	4	5	6	7	8	9	10
Low									High

Overall Mood									
1	2	3	4	5	6	7	8	9	10
Very Bad									Excellent

TUESDAY

Overall Anxiety Level									
1	2	3	4	5	6	7	8	9	10
Low									High

Overall Mood									
1	2	3	4	5	6	7	8	9	10
Very Bad									Excellent

WEDNESDAY

Overall Anxiety Level									
1	2	3	4	5	6	7	8	9	10
Low									High

Overall Mood									
1	2	3	4	5	6	7	8	9	10
Very Bad									Excellent

THURSDAY

Overall Anxiety Level									
1	2	3	4	5	6	7	8	9	10
Low									High

Overall Mood									
1	2	3	4	5	6	7	8	9	10
Very Bad									Excellent

WEEK OF _____ / ____ / ____

FRIDAY	Overall Anxiety Level									
	1	2	3	4	5	6	7	8	9	10
	Low									High
	Overall Mood									
	1	2	3	4	5	6	7	8	9	10
	Very Bad									Excellent

SATURDAY	Overall Anxiety Level									
	1	2	3	4	5	6	7	8	9	10
	Low									High
	Overall Mood									
	1	2	3	4	5	6	7	8	9	10
	Very Bad									Excellent

SUNDAY	Overall Anxiety Level									
	1	2	3	4	5	6	7	8	9	10
	Low									High
	Overall Mood									
	1	2	3	4	5	6	7	8	9	10
	Very Bad									Excellent

NOTES

_____

_____

_____

_____

_____

_____

Self Care Checklist

ACTIVITY	M	T	W	T	F	S	S
SPIRITUAL							
PYSICAL							
MENTAL							

Describe something
you need to forgive
yourself for. Then
forgive yourself.

DATE: _____ / _____ /
_____

Anxiety Triggers

When this happens:

| |
| |

This is what I think:

| |
| |

This is how I feel:

| |
| |

What I can do in this event to reduce my anxiety:

| |
| |

Anxiety Worksheet

DATE: _____ / _____ / _____

What happened?

What were my thoughts?

How did I handle it?

How did I feel?

What can I do to improve?

Anxiety Worksheet

DATE: ____ / ____ / ____

What happened?

What were my thoughts?	How did I feel?

How did I handle it?

What can I do to improve?

Exercise to Calm Down

B·R·E·A·T·H·E

5 Things I Can See

1.

2.

3.

4.

5.

4 Things I Can Touch

1.

2.

3.

4.

3 Things I Can Hear

1.

2.

3.

2 Things I Can Smell

1.

2.

1 Thing I Can Taste

1.

"If you always do what you've always done, you'll always get what you've always got."
~ Steven Hayes

Weekly Anxiety Tracker

MONDAY	Overall Anxiety Level
	1 2 3 4 5 6 7 8 9 10
	Low High
	Overall Mood
	1 2 3 4 5 6 7 8 9 10
	Very Bad Excellent

TUESDAY	Overall Anxiety Level
	1 2 3 4 5 6 7 8 9 10
	Low High
	Overall Mood
	1 2 3 4 5 6 7 8 9 10
	Very Bad Excellent

WEDNESDAY	Overall Anxiety Level
	1 2 3 4 5 6 7 8 9 10
	Low High
	Overall Mood
	1 2 3 4 5 6 7 8 9 10
	Very Bad Excellent

THURSDAY	Overall Anxiety Level
	1 2 3 4 5 6 7 8 9 10
	Low High
	Overall Mood
	1 2 3 4 5 6 7 8 9 10
	Very Bad Excellent

FRIDAY	Overall Anxiety Level									
	1	2	3	4	5	6	7	8	9	10
	Low									High
	Overall Mood									
	1	2	3	4	5	6	7	8	9	10
	Very Bad									Excellent

SATURDAY	Overall Anxiety Level									
	1	2	3	4	5	6	7	8	9	10
	Low									High
	Overall Mood									
	1	2	3	4	5	6	7	8	9	10
	Very Bad									Excellent

SUNDAY	Overall Anxiety Level									
	1	2	3	4	5	6	7	8	9	10
	Low									High
	Overall Mood									
	1	2	3	4	5	6	7	8	9	10
	Very Bad									Excellent

NOTES

Self Care Checklist

ACTIVITY	M	T	W	T	F	S	S
SPIRITUAL							
PYSICAL							
MENTAL							

Write about ten
things that you are
grateful for.

DATE: _____ / _____ /
_____

Anxiety Triggers

When this happens:

This is what I think:

This is how I feel:

What I can do in this event to reduce my anxiety:

Anxiety Worksheet

DATE: _____ / _____ / _____

What happened?

What were my thoughts?

How did I handle it?

How did I feel?

What can I do to improve?

Anxiety Worksheet

DATE: ____ / ____ / ____

What happened?

What were my thoughts?	How did I feel?

How did I handle it?

What can I do to improve?

Exercise to Calm Down
B·R·E·A·T·H·E

5 Things I Can See

1.

2.

3.

4.

5.

4 Things I Can Touch

1.

2.

3.

4.

3 Things I Can Hear

1.

2.

3.

2 Things I Can Smell

1.

2.

1 Thing I Can Taste

1.

"You don't have to control your thoughts. You just have to stop letting them control you."

~ Dan Millman

Weekly Anxiety Tracker

MONDAY											
	Overall Anxiety Level										
	1	2	3	4	5	6	7	8	9	10	
	Low									High	
	Overall Mood										
	1	2	3	4	5	6	7	8	9	10	
	Very Bad									Excellent	

TUESDAY											
	Overall Anxiety Level										
	1	2	3	4	5	6	7	8	9	10	
	Low									High	
	Overall Mood										
	1	2	3	4	5	6	7	8	9	10	
	Very Bad									Excellent	

WEDNESDAY											
	Overall Anxiety Level										
	1	2	3	4	5	6	7	8	9	10	
	Low									High	
	Overall Mood										
	1	2	3	4	5	6	7	8	9	10	
	Very Bad									Excellent	

THURSDAY											
	Overall Anxiety Level										
	1	2	3	4	5	6	7	8	9	10	
	Low									High	
	Overall Mood										
	1	2	3	4	5	6	7	8	9	10	
	Very Bad									Excellent	

WEEK OF _____ / ____ / ____

FRIDAY	Overall Anxiety Level
	1 2 3 4 5 6 7 8 9 10
	Low High
	Overall Mood
	1 2 3 4 5 6 7 8 9 10
	Very Bad Excellent

SATURDAY	Overall Anxiety Level
	1 2 3 4 5 6 7 8 9 10
	Low High
	Overall Mood
	1 2 3 4 5 6 7 8 9 10
	Very Bad Excellent

SUNDAY	Overall Anxiety Level
	1 2 3 4 5 6 7 8 9 10
	Low High
	Overall Mood
	1 2 3 4 5 6 7 8 9 10
	Very Bad Excellent

NOTES

_____

_____

_____

_____

_____

_____

Self Care Checklist

ACTIVITY	M	T	W	T	F	S	S
SPIRITUAL							
PYSICAL							
MENTAL							

Describe a difficult
situation you
overcame in the past.

DATE: _____ / _____ / _____

_____

_____

_____

_____

_____

_____

_____

_____

_____

_____

_____

_____

_____

_____

_____

_____

Anxiety Triggers

When this happens:

This is what I think:

This is how I feel:

What I can do in this event to reduce my anxiety:

Anxiety Worksheet

DATE: _____ / _____ / _____

What happened?

What were my thoughts?

How did I handle it?

How did I feel?

What can I do to improve?

Anxiety Worksheet

DATE: _____ / _____ / _____

What happened?

What were my thoughts?	How did I feel?

How did I handle it?

What can I do to improve?

Exercise to Calm Down
B·R·E·A·T·H·E

5 Things I Can See

1.

2.

3.

4.

5.

4 Things I Can Touch

1.

2.

3.

4.

3 Things I Can Hear

1.

2.

3.

2 Things I Can Smell

1.

2.

1 Thing I Can Taste

1.

"Smile,
Breathe, and
Go slowly."
~ Thich Nhat Hanh

Weekly Anxiety Tracker

MONDAY	Overall Anxiety Level									
	1	2	3	4	5	6	7	8	9	10
	Low									High
	Overall Mood									
	1	2	3	4	5	6	7	8	9	10
	Very Bad									Excellent

TUESDAY	Overall Anxiety Level									
	1	2	3	4	5	6	7	8	9	10
	Low									High
	Overall Mood									
	1	2	3	4	5	6	7	8	9	10
	Very Bad									Excellent

WEDNESDAY	Overall Anxiety Level									
	1	2	3	4	5	6	7	8	9	10
	Low									High
	Overall Mood									
	1	2	3	4	5	6	7	8	9	10
	Very Bad									Excellent

THURSDAY	Overall Anxiety Level									
	1	2	3	4	5	6	7	8	9	10
	Low									High
	Overall Mood									
	1	2	3	4	5	6	7	8	9	10
	Very Bad									Excellent

WEEK OF _____ / _____ / _____

FRIDAY	Overall Anxiety Level
	1 2 3 4 5 6 7 8 9 10
	Low High
	Overall Mood
	1 2 3 4 5 6 7 8 9 10
	Very Bad Excellent

SATURDAY	Overall Anxiety Level
	1 2 3 4 5 6 7 8 9 10
	Low High
	Overall Mood
	1 2 3 4 5 6 7 8 9 10
	Very Bad Excellent

SUNDAY	Overall Anxiety Level
	1 2 3 4 5 6 7 8 9 10
	Low High
	Overall Mood
	1 2 3 4 5 6 7 8 9 10
	Very Bad Excellent

NOTES

_____

_____

_____

_____

_____

_____

Self Care Checklist

ACTIVITY	M	T	W	T	F	S	S
SPIRITUAL							
PYSICAL							
MENTAL							

List five most
important things you
must get done this
week.

DATE: _____ / _____ /
_____

Anxiety Triggers

When this happens:

```
┌─────────────────────────────────────────────────────────┐
│                                                         │
│                                                         │
│                                                         │
│                                                         │
└─────────────────────────────────────────────────────────┘
```

This is what I think: This is how I feel:

```
┌──────────────────────────┐      ┌──────────────────────────┐
│                          │      │                          │
│                          │      │                          │
│                          │      │                          │
│                          │      │                          │
│                          │      │                          │
│                          │      │                          │
│                          │      │                          │
└──────────────────────────┘      └──────────────────────────┘
```

What I can do in this event to reduce my anxiety:

```
┌─────────────────────────────────────────────────────────┐
│                                                         │
│                                                         │
│                                                         │
│                                                         │
│                                                         │
└─────────────────────────────────────────────────────────┘
```

Anxiety Worksheet

DATE: _____ / _____ / _____

What happened?

What were my thoughts?

How did I handle it?

How did I feel?

What can I do to improve?

Anxiety Worksheet

DATE: _____ / _____ / _____

What happened?

What were my thoughts?	How did I feel?

How did I handle it?

What can I do to improve?

Exercise to Calm Down
B·R·E·A·T·H·E

5 Things I Can See

1.

2.

3.

4.

5.

4 Things I Can Touch

1.

2.

3.

4.

3 Things I Can Hear

1.

2.

3.

2 Things I Can Smell

1.

2.

1 Thing I Can Taste

1.

"You can't
always control what
goes on outside.
But you can always control
what goes on inside."
~ Wayne Dyer

Weekly Anxiety Tracker

MONDAY

	Overall Anxiety Level									
	1	2	3	4	5	6	7	8	9	10
	Low									High

	Overall Mood									
	1	2	3	4	5	6	7	8	9	10
	Very Bad									Excellent

TUESDAY

	Overall Anxiety Level									
	1	2	3	4	5	6	7	8	9	10
	Low									High

	Overall Mood									
	1	2	3	4	5	6	7	8	9	10
	Very Bad									Excellent

WEDNESDAY

	Overall Anxiety Level									
	1	2	3	4	5	6	7	8	9	10
	Low									High

	Overall Mood									
	1	2	3	4	5	6	7	8	9	10
	Very Bad									Excellent

THURSDAY

	Overall Anxiety Level									
	1	2	3	4	5	6	7	8	9	10
	Low									High

	Overall Mood									
	1	2	3	4	5	6	7	8	9	10
	Very Bad									Excellent

WEEK OF _____ / ____ / ____

FRIDAY	Overall Anxiety Level									
	1	2	3	4	5	6	7	8	9	10
	Low									High
	Overall Mood									
	1	2	3	4	5	6	7	8	9	10
	Very Bad									Excellent

SATURDAY	Overall Anxiety Level									
	1	2	3	4	5	6	7	8	9	10
	Low									High
	Overall Mood									
	1	2	3	4	5	6	7	8	9	10
	Very Bad									Excellent

SUNDAY	Overall Anxiety Level									
	1	2	3	4	5	6	7	8	9	10
	Low									High
	Overall Mood									
	1	2	3	4	5	6	7	8	9	10
	Very Bad									Excellent

NOTES

_____

_____

_____

_____

_____

_____

Self Care Checklist

ACTIVITY	M	T	W	T	F	S	S
SPIRITUAL							
PYSICAL							
MENTAL							

Name something that
triggers anxiety and
brainstorm some ideas
for handling this trigger.

DATE: _____ / _____ /
_____

Anxiety Triggers

When this happens:

This is what I think:

This is how I feel:

What I can do in this event to reduce my anxiety:

Anxiety Worksheet

DATE: _____ / _____ / _____

What happened?

What were my thoughts?

How did I handle it?

How did I feel?

What can I do to improve?

Anxiety Worksheet

DATE: ____ / ____ / ____

What happened?

What were my thoughts?	How did I feel?

How did I handle it?

What can I do to improve?

Exercise to Calm Down

B·R·E·A·T·H·E

5 Things I Can See

1.

2.

3.

4.

5.

4 Things I Can Touch

1.

2.

3.

4.

3 Things I Can Hear

1.

2.

3.

2 Things I Can Smell

1.

2.

1 Thing I Can Taste

1.

"Every time you are tempted
to react in the
same old way,
ask if you want to
be a prisoner of the past
or a pioneer of the future."
~ Deepak Chopra

Weekly Anxiety Tracker

MONDAY	Overall Anxiety Level
	1 2 3 4 5 6 7 8 9 10
	Low High
	Overall Mood
	1 2 3 4 5 6 7 8 9 10
	Very Bad Excellent

TUESDAY	Overall Anxiety Level
	1 2 3 4 5 6 7 8 9 10
	Low High
	Overall Mood
	1 2 3 4 5 6 7 8 9 10
	Very Bad Excellent

WEDNESDAY	Overall Anxiety Level
	1 2 3 4 5 6 7 8 9 10
	Low High
	Overall Mood
	1 2 3 4 5 6 7 8 9 10
	Very Bad Excellent

THURSDAY	Overall Anxiety Level
	1 2 3 4 5 6 7 8 9 10
	Low High
	Overall Mood
	1 2 3 4 5 6 7 8 9 10
	Very Bad Excellent

WEEK OF ____ / ____ / ____

FRIDAY	Overall Anxiety Level									
	1	2	3	4	5	6	7	8	9	10
	Low									High
	Overall Mood									
	1	2	3	4	5	6	7	8	9	10
	Very Bad									Excellent

SATURDAY	Overall Anxiety Level									
	1	2	3	4	5	6	7	8	9	10
	Low									High
	Overall Mood									
	1	2	3	4	5	6	7	8	9	10
	Very Bad									Excellent

SUNDAY	Overall Anxiety Level									
	1	2	3	4	5	6	7	8	9	10
	Low									High
	Overall Mood									
	1	2	3	4	5	6	7	8	9	10
	Very Bad									Excellent

NOTES

_____

_____

_____

_____

_____

_____

Self Care Checklist

ACTIVITY	M	T	W	T	F	S	S
SPIRITUAL							
PYSICAL							
MENTAL							

Make a five-year goal for
your life, then brainstorm
ideas and make plans to
achieve it.

DATE: _____ / _____ /
_____

Anxiety Triggers

When this happens:

This is what I think:

This is how I feel:

What I can do in this event to reduce my anxiety:

Anxiety Worksheet

DATE: _____ / _____ / _____

What happened?

What were my thoughts?

How did I handle it?

How did I feel?

What can I do to improve?

Anxiety Worksheet

DATE: ____ / ____ / ____

What happened?

What were my thoughts?	How did I feel?

How did I handle it?

What can I do to improve?

Exercise to Calm Down
B · R · E · A · T · H · E

5 Things I Can See

1. _____

2. _____

3. _____

4. _____

5. _____

4 Things I Can Touch

1. _____

2. _____

3. _____

4. _____

3 Things I Can Hear

1. _____

2. _____

3. _____

2 Things I Can Smell

1. _____

2. _____

1 Thing I Can Taste

1. _____

"Anxiety does not empty tomorrow of its sorrows, but only empties today of its strength."
~ Charles Spurgeon

Weekly Anxiety Tracker

MONDAY

Overall Anxiety Level
1   2   3   4   5   6   7   8   9   10
Low   High

Overall Mood
1   2   3   4   5   6   7   8   9   10
Very Bad   Excellent

TUESDAY

Overall Anxiety Level
1   2   3   4   5   6   7   8   9   10
Low   High

Overall Mood
1   2   3   4   5   6   7   8   9   10
Very Bad   Excellent

WEDNESDAY

Overall Anxiety Level
1   2   3   4   5   6   7   8   9   10
Low   High

Overall Mood
1   2   3   4   5   6   7   8   9   10
Very Bad   Excellent

THURSDAY

Overall Anxiety Level
1   2   3   4   5   6   7   8   9   10
Low   High

Overall Mood
1   2   3   4   5   6   7   8   9   10
Very Bad   Excellent

WEEK OF _____ / ____ / ____

FRIDAY

	Overall Anxiety Level

Overall Anxiety Level

1	2	3	4	5	6	7	8	9	10

Low   High

Overall Mood

1	2	3	4	5	6	7	8	9	10

Very Bad   Excellent

SATURDAY

Overall Anxiety Level

1	2	3	4	5	6	7	8	9	10

Low   High

Overall Mood

1	2	3	4	5	6	7	8	9	10

Very Bad   Excellent

SUNDAY

Overall Anxiety Level

1	2	3	4	5	6	7	8	9	10

Low   High

Overall Mood

1	2	3	4	5	6	7	8	9	10

Very Bad   Excellent

NOTES

_____

_____

_____

_____

_____

_____

Self Care Checklist

ACTIVITY	M	T	W	T	F	S	S
SPIRITUAL							
PYSICAL							
MENTAL							

List three things that
you would do if
nothing scared you.

DATE: _____ / _____ /
_____

Anxiety Triggers

When this happens:

This is what I think:

This is how I feel:

What I can do in this event to reduce my anxiety:

Anxiety Worksheet

DATE: _____ / _____ / _____

What happened?

What were my thoughts?

How did I handle it?

How did I feel?

What can I do to improve?

Anxiety Worksheet

DATE: ____ / ____ / ____

What happened?

What were my thoughts?	How did I feel?

How did I handle it?

What can I do to improve?

Exercise to Calm Down
B·R·E·A·T·H·E

5 Things I Can See

1.

2.

3.

4.

5.

4 Things I Can Touch

1.

2.

3.

4.

3 Things I Can Hear

1.

2.

3.

2 Things I Can Smell

1.

2.

1 Thing I Can Taste

1.

"Every time you are tempted
to react in the
same old way,
ask if you want to
be a prisoner of the past
or a pioneer of the future."
~ Deepak Chopra

Weekly Anxiety Tracker

MONDAY

Overall Anxiety Level									
1	2	3	4	5	6	7	8	9	10
Low									High

Overall Mood									
1	2	3	4	5	6	7	8	9	10
Very Bad									Excellent

TUESDAY

Overall Anxiety Level									
1	2	3	4	5	6	7	8	9	10
Low									High

Overall Mood									
1	2	3	4	5	6	7	8	9	10
Very Bad									Excellent

WEDNESDAY

Overall Anxiety Level									
1	2	3	4	5	6	7	8	9	10
Low									High

Overall Mood									
1	2	3	4	5	6	7	8	9	10
Very Bad									Excellent

THURSDAY

Overall Anxiety Level									
1	2	3	4	5	6	7	8	9	10
Low									High

Overall Mood									
1	2	3	4	5	6	7	8	9	10
Very Bad									Excellent

WEEK OF _____ / ____ / ____

FRIDAY	Overall Anxiety Level									
	1	2	3	4	5	6	7	8	9	10
	Low									High
	Overall Mood									
	1	2	3	4	5	6	7	8	9	10
	Very Bad									Excellent

SATURDAY	Overall Anxiety Level									
	1	2	3	4	5	6	7	8	9	10
	Low									High
	Overall Mood									
	1	2	3	4	5	6	7	8	9	10
	Very Bad									Excellent

SUNDAY	Overall Anxiety Level									
	1	2	3	4	5	6	7	8	9	10
	Low									High
	Overall Mood									
	1	2	3	4	5	6	7	8	9	10
	Very Bad									Excellent

NOTES

_____

_____

_____

_____

_____

_____

Self Care Checklist

ACTIVITY	M	T	W	T	F	S	S
SPIRITUAL							
PYSICAL							
MENTAL							

Write down what the
word "Gratitude"
means to you.

DATE: _____ / _____ /
_____

_____

_____

_____

_____

_____

_____

_____

_____

_____

_____

_____

_____

_____

_____

_____

Anxiety Triggers

When this happens:

| |
| |

This is what I think:

This is how I feel:

| | |
| | |

What I can do in this event to reduce my anxiety:

| |
| |

Anxiety Worksheet

DATE: _____ / _____ / _____

What happened?

What were my thoughts?

How did I handle it?

How did I feel?

What can I do to improve?

Anxiety Worksheet

DATE: ____ / ____ / ____

What happened?

What were my thoughts?	How did I feel?

How did I handle it?

What can I do to improve?

Exercise to Calm Down

B·R·E·A·T·H·E

5 Things I Can See

1. _____

2. _____

3. _____

4. _____

5. _____

4 Things I Can Touch

1. _____

2. _____

3. _____

4. _____

3 Things I Can Hear

1. _____

2. _____

3. _____

2 Things I Can Smell

1. _____

2. _____

1 Thing I Can Taste

1. _____

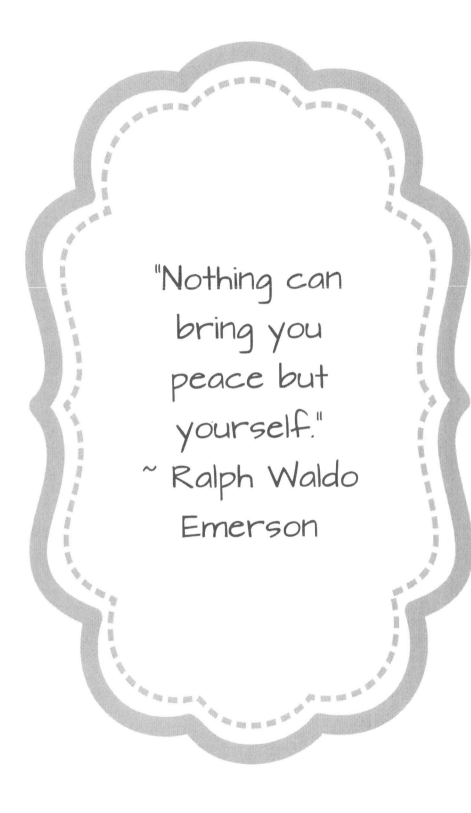

"Nothing can bring you peace but yourself." ~ Ralph Waldo Emerson

Weekly Anxiety Tracker

MONDAY	Overall Anxiety Level
	1 2 3 4 5 6 7 8 9 10
	Low High
	Overall Mood
	1 2 3 4 5 6 7 8 9 10
	Very Bad Excellent

TUESDAY	Overall Anxiety Level
	1 2 3 4 5 6 7 8 9 10
	Low High
	Overall Mood
	1 2 3 4 5 6 7 8 9 10
	Very Bad Excellent

WEDNESDAY	Overall Anxiety Level
	1 2 3 4 5 6 7 8 9 10
	Low High
	Overall Mood
	1 2 3 4 5 6 7 8 9 10
	Very Bad Excellent

THURSDAY	Overall Anxiety Level
	1 2 3 4 5 6 7 8 9 10
	Low High
	Overall Mood
	1 2 3 4 5 6 7 8 9 10
	Very Bad Excellent

WEEK OF _____ / ____ / ____

FRIDAY	Overall Anxiety Level
	1 2 3 4 5 6 7 8 9 10
	Low High
	Overall Mood
	1 2 3 4 5 6 7 8 9 10
	Very Bad Excellent

SATURDAY	Overall Anxiety Level
	1 2 3 4 5 6 7 8 9 10
	Low High
	Overall Mood
	1 2 3 4 5 6 7 8 9 10
	Very Bad Excellent

SUNDAY	Overall Anxiety Level
	1 2 3 4 5 6 7 8 9 10
	Low High
	Overall Mood
	1 2 3 4 5 6 7 8 9 10
	Very Bad Excellent

NOTES

_____

_____

_____

_____

_____

_____

Self Care Checklist

ACTIVITY	M	T	W	T	F	S	S
SPIRITUAL							
PYSICAL							
MENTAL							

What is your favorite
memory?

DATE: _____ / _____ /
_____

_____

_____

_____

_____

_____

_____

_____

_____

_____

_____

_____

_____

_____

_____

_____

Anxiety Triggers

When this happens:

This is what I think:

This is how I feel:

What I can do in this event to reduce my anxiety:

Anxiety Worksheet

DATE: _____ / _____ / _____

What happened?

What were my thoughts?

How did I handle it?

How did I feel?

What can I do to improve?

Anxiety Worksheet

DATE: _____ / _____ / _____

What happened?

What were my thoughts?	How did I feel?

How did I handle it?

What can I do to improve?

Exercise to Calm Down

B·R·E·A·T·H·E

5 Things I Can See

1. _____

2. _____

3. _____

4. _____

5. _____

4 Things I Can Touch

1. _____

2. _____

3. _____

4. _____

3 Things I Can Hear

1. _____

2. _____

3. _____

2 Things I Can Smell

1. _____

2. _____

1 Thing I Can Taste

1. _____

"Hey you, keep living. It won't always be this overwhelming."
— Jacqueline Whitney

Weekly Anxiety Tracker

MONDAY

	Overall Anxiety Level
	1 2 3 4 5 6 7 8 9 10
	Low High
	Overall Mood
	1 2 3 4 5 6 7 8 9 10
	Very Bad Excellent

TUESDAY

	Overall Anxiety Level
	1 2 3 4 5 6 7 8 9 10
	Low High
	Overall Mood
	1 2 3 4 5 6 7 8 9 10
	Very Bad Excellent

WEDNESDAY

	Overall Anxiety Level
	1 2 3 4 5 6 7 8 9 10
	Low High
	Overall Mood
	1 2 3 4 5 6 7 8 9 10
	Very Bad Excellent

THURSDAY

	Overall Anxiety Level
	1 2 3 4 5 6 7 8 9 10
	Low High
	Overall Mood
	1 2 3 4 5 6 7 8 9 10
	Very Bad Excellent

WEEK OF _____ / ____ / ____

FRIDAY	Overall Anxiety Level
	1 2 3 4 5 6 7 8 9 10
	Low High
	Overall Mood
	1 2 3 4 5 6 7 8 9 10
	Very Bad Excellent

SATURDAY	Overall Anxiety Level
	1 2 3 4 5 6 7 8 9 10
	Low High
	Overall Mood
	1 2 3 4 5 6 7 8 9 10
	Very Bad Excellent

SUNDAY	Overall Anxiety Level
	1 2 3 4 5 6 7 8 9 10
	Low High
	Overall Mood
	1 2 3 4 5 6 7 8 9 10
	Very Bad Excellent

NOTES

_____

_____

_____

_____

_____

_____

Self Care Checklist

ACTIVITY	M	T	W	T	F	S	S
SPIRITUAL							
PYSICAL							
MENTAL							

Describe the things
that make you feel
better after a bad
day.

DATE: _____ / _____ /
_____

Anxiety Triggers

When this happens:

[ ]

This is what I think:

[ ]

This is how I feel:

[ ]

What I can do in this event to reduce my anxiety:

[ ]

Anxiety Worksheet

DATE: _____ / _____ / _____

What happened?

What were my thoughts?

How did I handle it?

How did I feel?

What can I do to improve?

Anxiety Worksheet

DATE: ____ / ____ / ____

What happened?

What were my thoughts?	How did I feel?

How did I handle it?

What can I do to improve?

Exercise to Calm Down
B·R·E·A·T·H·E

5 Things I Can See

1.

2.

3.

4.

5.

4 Things I Can Touch

1.

2.

3.

4.

3 Things I Can Hear

1.

2.

3.

2 Things I Can Smell

1.

2.

1 Thing I Can Taste

1.

"Sometimes the most important thing in a whole day is the rest taken between two deep breaths."
— Etty Hillesum

Weekly Anxiety Tracker

MONDAY

Overall Anxiety Level									
1	2	3	4	5	6	7	8	9	10
Low									High

Overall Mood									
1	2	3	4	5	6	7	8	9	10
Very Bad									Excellent

TUESDAY

Overall Anxiety Level									
1	2	3	4	5	6	7	8	9	10
Low									High

Overall Mood									
1	2	3	4	5	6	7	8	9	10
Very Bad									Excellent

WEDNESDAY

Overall Anxiety Level									
1	2	3	4	5	6	7	8	9	10
Low									High

Overall Mood									
1	2	3	4	5	6	7	8	9	10
Very Bad									Excellent

THURSDAY

Overall Anxiety Level									
1	2	3	4	5	6	7	8	9	10
Low									High

Overall Mood									
1	2	3	4	5	6	7	8	9	10
Very Bad									Excellent

WEEK OF _____ / ____ / ____

FRIDAY

Overall Anxiety Level									
1	2	3	4	5	6	7	8	9	10
Low									High

Overall Mood									
1	2	3	4	5	6	7	8	9	10
Very Bad									Excellent

SATURDAY

Overall Anxiety Level									
1	2	3	4	5	6	7	8	9	10
Low									High

Overall Mood									
1	2	3	4	5	6	7	8	9	10
Very Bad									Excellent

SUNDAY

Overall Anxiety Level									
1	2	3	4	5	6	7	8	9	10
Low									High

Overall Mood									
1	2	3	4	5	6	7	8	9	10
Very Bad									Excellent

NOTES

Self Care Checklist

ACTIVITY	M	T	W	T	F	S	S
SPIRITUAL							
PYSICAL							
MENTAL							

Write about a recent
challenge you have
overcome, big or small,
and how that victory
made you feel.

DATE: _____ / _____ /
_____

_____

_____

_____

_____

_____

_____

_____

_____

_____

_____

_____

_____

_____

_____

_____

Anxiety Triggers

When this happens:

This is what I think:

This is how I feel:

What I can do in this event to reduce my anxiety:

Anxiety Worksheet

DATE: _____ / _____ / _____

What happened?

What were my thoughts?

How did I handle it?

How did I feel?

What can I do to improve?

Anxiety Worksheet

DATE: ____ / ____ / ____

What happened?

What were my thoughts?	How did I feel?

How did I handle it?

What can I do to improve?

Exercise to Calm Down
B·R·E·A·T·H·E

5 Things I Can See

1.

2.

3.

4.

5.

4 Things I Can Touch

1.

2.

3.

4.

3 Things I Can Hear

1.

2.

3.

2 Things I Can Smell

1.

2.

1 Thing I Can Taste

1.

"Every tomorrow has two handles. We can take hold of it with the handle of anxiety or the handle of faith."

– Henry Ward Beecher

Weekly Anxiety Tracker

MONDAY

Overall Anxiety Level

1   2   3   4   5   6   7   8   9   10

Low   High

Overall Mood

1   2   3   4   5   6   7   8   9   10

Very Bad   Excellent

TUESDAY

Overall Anxiety Level

1   2   3   4   5   6   7   8   9   10

Low   High

Overall Mood

1   2   3   4   5   6   7   8   9   10

Very Bad   Excellent

WEDNESDAY

Overall Anxiety Level

1   2   3   4   5   6   7   8   9   10

Low   High

Overall Mood

1   2   3   4   5   6   7   8   9   10

Very Bad   Excellent

THURSDAY

Overall Anxiety Level

1   2   3   4   5   6   7   8   9   10

Low   High

Overall Mood

1   2   3   4   5   6   7   8   9   10

Very Bad   Excellent

WEEK OF _____ / ____ / ____

FRIDAY	Overall Anxiety Level									
	1	2	3	4	5	6	7	8	9	10
	Low									High
	Overall Mood									
	1	2	3	4	5	6	7	8	9	10
	Very Bad									Excellent

SATURDAY	Overall Anxiety Level									
	1	2	3	4	5	6	7	8	9	10
	Low									High
	Overall Mood									
	1	2	3	4	5	6	7	8	9	10
	Very Bad									Excellent

SUNDAY	Overall Anxiety Level									
	1	2	3	4	5	6	7	8	9	10
	Low									High
	Overall Mood									
	1	2	3	4	5	6	7	8	9	10
	Very Bad									Excellent

NOTES

Self Care Checklist

ACTIVITY	M	T	W	T	F	S	S
SPIRITUAL							
PYSICAL							
MENTAL							

Describe your most
memorable vacation.

DATE: _____ / _____ /
_____

Anxiety Triggers

When this happens:

This is what I think:

This is how I feel:

What I can do in this event to reduce my anxiety:

Anxiety Worksheet

DATE: _____ / _____ / _____

What happened?

What were my thoughts?

How did I handle it?

How did I feel?

What can I do to improve?

Anxiety Worksheet

DATE: _____ / _____ / _____

What happened?

What were my thoughts?	How did I feel?

How did I handle it?

What can I do to improve?

Exercise to Calm Down
B·R·E·A·T·H·E

5 Things I Can See

1.

2.

3.

4.

5.

4 Things I Can Touch

1.

2.

3.

4.

3 Things I Can Hear

1.

2.

3.

2 Things I Can Smell

1.

2.

1 Thing I Can Taste

1.

Write down what the word
"Joy" means to you and list
the people or things that
bring you joy.

DATE: _____ / _____ /
_____

Make a list of at
least five kind things
to say to yourself
every day.

DATE: _____ / _____ /
_____

What is your biggest
accomplishment in the last
year? What did you do to
achieve it and how did it
make you feel?

DATE: _____ / _____ /
_____

Make a list of songs
that make you feel
happy.

DATE: _____ / _____ /
_____

Describe where you would go if you could go anywhere for vacation. Why? What would you do there?

DATE: _____ / _____ / _____

_____

_____

_____

_____

_____

_____

_____

_____

_____

_____

_____

_____

_____

_____

Printed in Great Britain
by Amazon